INTRODUCTION

Frome is a very special town, a place of g
exceptional architectural heritage is largely th
of the clothing industry, but later industries
malting and brewing, have also contributed t
contains three Conservation Areas, design.
outstanding architectural and historic character.

....ance its

EARLY DAYS

Frome has developed from an early religious foundation. In about 685 AD St Aldhelm founded a church here, the direct predecessor of the present St John's. Frome was an important royal estate in the Saxon period and in 934 King Athelstan held a witengamot or great council here, attended by great men of the realm: the Archbishops of York and Canterbury, thirteen bishops and numerous princes, earls and thegns. In 955 King Edred died at Frome.

Frome was the focus of Frome Hundred, although the hundred court met at a long barrow, known as Modbury or Big Tree, on Buckland Down. It was one of the largest Saxon administrative units in Somerset and was later split into the three separate hundreds of Frome, Wellow and Kilmersdon. Such a great estate, which the presence of kings and great noble men attested, seems certain to have had a royal palace, perhaps similar to the one which has been excavated at Cheddar.

Frome was already a centre with some urban functions by the 11th century, when the Domesday Book records a valuable market, however there is no mention of burgesses, holders of formal urban burgage tenure plots, and it is the agricultural character of the manor of Frome which is the overwhelming impression gained from the Domesday entry.

Frome ceased to be a royal estate when Henry I granted it to Roger de Courcelles in the 12th century. The main manor descended through the families of FitzBernard (1215-38), Branch (1238-1349), Wynslade (1361-1405), Leversedge (c1405-1706) and Seaman (1706-51), before the Earl of Cork and Orrery of nearby Marston Bigot. The manorial dwelling, from at least the 13th century, was situated well outside the town, at Vallis.

THE TRAIL

Follow the route descriptions in italics in conjunction with the map.

The Trail is linked to a series of numbered plaques generously sponsored by the Frome Selwood Permanent Building Society in celebration of Frome's 1300th anniversary in 1985. The Frome Selwood has since been taken over by the Coventry Building Society. The trail starts outside of the Round Tower, Justice Lane.

The Round Tower was built as a wool-drying stove, probably in the 18th century, and stood in a ruinous condition for many years, until renovated in 1994. Another tower stands tucked away behind houses in Willow Vale and a third stands at Buckland Dinham.

3

Round Tower

The area facing the Round Tower used to be the Cattle Market, until the market was moved to Standerwick in 1990. The large building which lies on the far side of the Cattle Market was once the Market Hall now usually called the Cheese and Grain. In the past cheese and other products were loaded onto trains on a railway siding at the rear of the building. Market House is a delightful building on the corner of Bridge Street which was the home of the market bailiff; it dates from the mid 18th century.

Turn right out of the gates of the courtyard and turn right again at the corner, stopping outside the Black Swan gallery.

The Black Swan, at one time an inn, is a lively arts centre which provides a sales outlet and exhibition space for a wide range of local artists and craftspeople, together with a cafe/restaurant which specialises in wholefood cuisine.

Walk on to the bridge over the River Frome. The river flows through the centre of Frome; it rises about nine miles away, in the parish of Brewham and flows north east to join the Avon at Freshford. When the local clothing industry was at its busiest, the Frome powered many fulling and corn mills. The course of the river as it runs alongside Willow Vale is part of a former millstream; the natural, winding course lay to the south of the Blue House.

The development of the wool and cloth industry during the Middle Ages brought growth and prosperity to Frome and to many surrounding villages. The homes of wealthy clothiers of the 17th and 18th centuries and the humbler dwellings of cloth workers are evidence of the area's economic heyday. During the Napoleonic wars Frome was famous for its blue cloth used for army uniforms. Woad was grown locally to produce the blue dye. Important local trades linked to textile production were those of card-making, dyeing, machinery and boiler manufacture.

With the industrial revolution came many changes, among which was the advent of purpose-built industrial buildings - factories, workshops and warehouses. The gathering together of clothworkers into industrial premises was an economic development which brought with it profound social change. In earlier times cloth production had been very much a family affair, taking place within the home, often with all members of the family involved in the process. Employment in factories broke the ancient link between family unit and production. It removed

4

Frome Museum

the freedom to combine clothworking with other part-time employment. Women and children, being cheaper, were favoured above men as employees for many tasks, leaving less-skilled men unable to find employment.

The Somerset and Wiltshire clothing industry failed to compete effectively with the textile producers of the north of England and from the early 19th century the local industry quickly declined, although Frome retained a woollen mill until 1965.

Silk production was an industry of some importance in a number of towns and villages of the area in the second half of the 19th century. At Merchants Barton, a silk mill was taken over in 1845 by William Thompson, from London. By 1851 the business employed over 300 women and children; he entered a partnership with Philip le Gros and they operated a second factory at Shepton Mallet; production at Merchants Barton finished in 1926.

Plaque 1 *The Corner of Willow Vale and North Parade.*

The bridge was built in 1667 and is a rare example of an English bridge with buildings on it, which date from 1821. Standing on the bridge, look left: the wedge-shaped building on the corner of North Parade and Bridge Street is now home to the Frome Museum, and was built in 1868 as the Literary and Scientific Institution, the gift of John Sinkins, a clothier. North Parade itself is an example of late 18th century town planning, an important element in Frome's development and present character. The delightful riverside road is Willow Vale (or Pilly Vale). A walk along this road will take you past an unexpected variety of buildings including some historic industrial premises, a maltings, dyehouse, wool drying tower,

Frome Bridge

5

an important 18th century clothing workshop which later became the feather factory, and some elegant clothiers houses. In several cases the humbler buildings or former workshops adjoin the fine houses built for prosperous dyers and clothiers.

The Blue House stands on a small island and is one of the finest buildings in Frome. The present building dates from 1724. The two wings each consisted of rooms for twelve old women, while the central portion was used as a charity school

Blue House

for twelve boys. The boys in bluecoat uniforms have given the building its name. The two figures on the façade are known as Nancy Guy and Billy Ball. The origins of the foundation date from 1461, when William Leversedge, Lord of the Manor

of Frome, founded an almshouse which consisted of a chapel and hall with twelve chambers, and endowed it with four and a half acres of land. A plaque installed by the Frome Society for Local Study tells the history of the building.

Plaque 2 *The Market Place. From the bridge, walk on to find the second plaque at Lloyds Bank in the Market Place.* The bank was rebuilt in 1874 for the Wilts and Dorset Bank. The initials of the architect J.W.Stent are found over the door. A

Boyle Cross

number of important and interesting buildings front on to the Market Place. The present National Westminster Bank was built in 1819 as a covered market with a ballroom above it.

The market was the centre of a mediaeval town and although livestock are no longer sold, a market is still held here on Wednesdays and Saturdays. In the Middle Ages Frome also had two fairs; the Frome Cheese Show which is held in September each year is the successor of these mediaeval events.

Cheap Street

Walk up mediaeval Cheap Street, where an ancient leat channels spring water down the centre of the pavement.

Most of the buildings date from the 16th and 17th century, however a fire in 1923 damaged a number of buildings; two are rare surviving examples of buildings jettied front and back. Number 11, the last but one shop on the left, was built circa 1500 and has carved Tudor roses on the beams inside the shop windows. The lamp which arches above Cheap Street was manufactured locally by Cockeys and was originally a gas lamp made in about 1890.

Plaque 3 *18 King Street.* The building which bears the plaque is 16th century, and is timber framed, although

Apple Alley

much altered. *Turn left at the top of Cheap Street and walk down King Street to look at the fine early 18th century building of Iron Gates, which lies straight ahead.* A fine moulded shell hood porch can be seen at the side of the building.

Walk back up the hill, stopping to look down Apple Alley which is a typical mediaeval alleyway. Further up the hill stop at the fountain which is fed by a spring which rises in the churchyard. Walk up Church Steps.

Via Crucis

The incongruous building on the corner of Eagle Lane and Church Steps occupies the site of the Mechanics Institute. Through the churchyard railings the fine carved stone Via Crucis created by the sculptor James Forsyth leads to the north porch where the Crucifixion is depicted. The Old Church House, 16th century, with a fine studded door and mullion and transom windows is on the right.

Cross the forecourt and walk up Bath Street to view Rook Lane Chapel.

The Act of Unconformity of 1662 imposed the Book of Common Prayer upon church congregations,

Rook Lane Chapel

Bath Street

and thereby laid the foundations of Frome's vigorous nonconformity. Dr Humfrey, minister at St John's, could not accept the Act and had to leave the living. He, with former members of St John's, formed the Rook Lane Congregation. Rook Lane Congregational Chapel was built in 1707 but the grandness of the building was offensive to some local people, the chapel being described as being 'as handsome perhaps as any in England, and there are few more spacious'. The cupola was especially provocative and it is recorded that in times of trouble a mob would gather and cry 'Down with the cupola'.

The fine row of cottages which lie below Rook Lane Chapel date from the 17th century. It is most unusual to find houses set back behind large front gardens so close to the centre of town; this has arisen through changes to the road system. Bath Street is not an ancient thoroughfare, but a part of the town's 19th century heritage, planned by Thomas Bunn, a local solicitor, benefactor and visionary; constructed after the 1810 Turnpike Act, it cut through the pre-existing street pattern. Bunn had many ambitious plans for Frome, and cherished the hope that it would one day be appropriate to write of 'Bath, near Frome'. The cedar tree dates from 1814 and is the sole survivor of a planting scheme of Bunn's.

Plaque 4 *Forecourt Screen of St John's. Returning to St John's church, notice the forecourt screen designed by Jeffry Wyatt later Sir Jeffry Wyatville.*

St John's was a 7th century foundation but the only Saxon fabric in the present church is represented by two carved stones, possibly part of a cross. The present building dates from 1160-70, but was largely rebuilt by the Tractarian vicar, WJ.E. Bennett, in 1856 -68.

Take the right hand path along the churchyard.

At the east end is the tomb of the saintly Thomas Ken, Bishop of Bath and Wells, who in 1691 refused to take an oath of allegiance to William and Mary, and was deprived of his living. He died at Longleat in 1711 leaving his silver chalice and paten to St John's.

At the end of the churchyard turn right. A little way up Blindhouse Lane notice the small oval window set high in the wall of the first building. These charming windows are a feature of 17th century buildings in Frome and several local villages.

Plaque 5 *Blindhouse Lane.*

The old lock-up, known as the Blind House, still survives in a corner of the churchyard. *Return back down Blindhouse Lane and turn right into Vicarage Street.* Number 33 Vicarage Street is 18th century, but the extension uphill is 17th century and was the Grammar School. Next door, the Auction Mart was built as a saleroom in 1865 and continues today.

Further along Vicarage Street, is a 15th century archway leading to a rear courtyard. This area once belonged to Cirencester Abbey and the archway led

Vicarage Street

to a tithe barn belonging to the monastery. Opposite the archway is the handsome vicarage, dated 1744, probably by Nathaniel Ireson.

Return along the path by the church to the bottom of Gentle Street.

Plaque 6 *Argyll House. Turn left up Gentle Street. A plaque installed by the Frome Society gives details.*

Argyll House was built in 1766 and contains a rare example of a Chinese Chippendale staircase. Oriel Lodge, next door, is later.

Oriel Lodge and Argyll House

The Chantry and Hermitage previously formed one house. The Hermitage still has a Phoenix insurance badge on the wall. Further up the hill is the Waggon and Horses, a former 17th century coaching inn from whose yard at the rear the 'Froome Flying Wagon' left for London. The journey took two days and cost one pound seven shillings (£1.35) per passenger. The last house on the right is 17th century, with characteristic gables and drip moulds over stone mullioned windows.

Rook Lane House

Plaque 7 *The former Lamb Brewery. At the top of the hill is an area known as Gorehedge (triangle in Old English). Turn right past the 19th century buildings of the former maltings and brewery.* The Lamb Brewery used to be on Gorehedge and the current buildings were a maltings later converted to a bottling stores.

Plaque 8 *Wesley Villas. Cross the road with great care and walk along Christchurch Street West.*

Wesley School and Villas

On the corner of Butts Hill and Christchurch Street West is a complex of 19th century buildings; the Wesleyan Methodist Church, with its associated manse, schoolroom and headmaster's house. On the right hand side of the road is Rook Lane House, built in 1600 for Robert Smith, a local clothier. The poet Elizabeth Rowe lived here as described on a plaque from the Frome Society. Opposite is a carved stone pillar; Thomas Bunn had a scheme for a crescent of Regency houses here.

Continue walking along Christchurch Street West. To the left, the present School of Dancing was built in 1857 as the town's police station. *Turn right down South Parade.* Note the old Friends Meeting House, founded in 1675. The Baptist Church beyond is dated 1850, and replaced the original from 1708. *Walk back up South Parade.* The Public Offices, 1891 in Christchurch Street West on the left are the only purpose built council offices in Frome. Rawlings carding factory is on the right. Further along stands Christ Church, built on Packhorse Field in 1818 for the 'labouring poor', where John Wesley preached on several occasions. Previously packhorses grazed after walking from Radstock loaded with coal, which was then delivered to the yard of the pub opposite. Adjoining the churchyard is the former Fire Station.

Plaque 9 *Wine Street. Turn right and walk down Wine Street.* It was developed in the 1730's by the Sheppards, the leading clothiers in Frome, who bought the land in 1652 for 22 pounds 10 shillings.

Plaque 10 *Sheppards Barton.* At the end of Wine Street is Sheppards Barton which was developed by the Sheppards to provide workshop and dwelling

Sheppards Barton Steps

accommodation for weavers. On the right hand side numbers 9-11 were built in 1840, much later than numbers 7 and 8, which were built about 1700 as one house. Numbers 2-6 were initially workshops for the weavers living in the cottages opposite. By 1820 mills at Spring Gardens, 2 miles from Frome, and Willow Vale were in operation and the workshops were converted into houses.

Catherine Hill

Plaque 11 *13 Catherine Hill.* The buildings on either side of the archway leading to Catherine Hill may have constituted a part of St Katherine's Chapel, known to exist in 1279, and dissolved in 1548. Well endowed, the Chapel owned all the land between Wine Street and the Trinity area. Note the blocked, pointed and arched window and the arch above the doorway of the right hand building. Two corbels still survive inside, and there is a wooden screen probably dating from the 1550's when the building was converted to secular use. It was once the home of John Sheppard, and in 1672 was licensed for use as a Baptist place of worship. The brick front elevation onto Catherine Hill dates from the widening of the street after the 1810 Turnpike Act.

A plaque from the Frome Society describes the history.

Turn right to walk down Catherine Hill. Catherine Hill was one of the main retail areas of Frome and has been revitalised and is a delightful place to shop, with a good range of arts and crafts, antiques, period clothes shops and businesses. Stony Street, between Catherine Hill and the Market Place, is another shopping street of great charm.

For the shorter route, walk down Stony Street to finish the trail in the Market Place. To follow the longer trail retrace your steps to the entrance to Sheppards Barton, then walk straight on up Catherine Hill. The Valentine Lamp is on your left, an addition to the special character of Catherine Hill. Catherine Hill House with its Doric pedimented doorway of the 18th century is situated behind older 17th century cottages. Further up the Catherine Street the imposing 19th century Doric portico formed the entrance to the Badcox Lane Baptist Church.

Plaque 12 *The Ship Inn. At the top of the hill is the 17th century Ship Inn, now called the 'Olive Tree'.Turn right along Vallis Way.* Above on the right you can see an 1890 representation of the four seasons on the fascia of the shops making Badcox Parade.

Trinity Street

Plaque 13 *38a Vallis Way.* The trail continues straight along Vallis Way but stop to look down Selwood Road, which was developed in the 1690s; many of the houses still have period gables.

Plaque 14 *1 Naish's Street.Turn down this road and walk down to the junction with Trinity Street.*

TRINITY

Trinity is of great historic importance as one of the earliest extensive developments of industrial housing in Western Europe. From 1665 a number of dwelling plots were laid out in enclosed fields adjacent to the town and houses for cloth workers were built. The development was speculative and was not for housing the employees of one clothier. Daniel Defoe, writing in the early 1720s noted that: 'The town of Froom is so prodigiously increased within these last twenty or thirty years, that they have built a new church, and so many new streets of houses, and those houses are so full of inhabitants, that Frome is now reckoned to have more people in it, than the city of Bath, and some say, than even Salisbury itself'.

An inventory of the Vallis Way home of John Jelly, clothier, made in 1724, gives a vivid picture of the internal arrangements of local houses at the time. On the ground floor was 'a kitchen, little inner room, hall, pantry, cellar, brewhouse', on the first floor 'a best chamber, kitchen chamber and a little chamber', and above were 'the garrotts and wool loft'. The 'sheare shop' was presumably a separate building within the curtilage. In most of the houses of the Trinity area an unheated downstairs chamber was used for cloth production, and in some homes upstairs chambers were also used in this way, probably also being used as bedrooms. *Continuing along the pedestrian way at the end of Naish's Street you reach Trinity Street.*

Plaque 15 *8 Trinity Street.* Trinity Street. was built between 1718 and 1722, when gables had gone out of fashion; Trinity Church (1838) stands at the top of the street. It contains some fine stained-glass windows designed by Burne-Jones, and executed by Morris & Co. At one time two inns stood on opposite sides of this road, the Bell Inn, and the Crown and Sceptre. An

Butler & Tanners Steam Printing Works

underground passage, using a natural fissure in the rock, leads to the Crown and Sceptre; it was used to bring beer from the brewery behind the Bell. *Walk right down Trinity Street to Selwood Road.* The 19th century former printing works of Butler and Tanner dominates the road junction.

BUTLER AND TANNER

The firm of Butler and Tanner has been of great importance in the employment history of Frome. Butler was a partner with William Langford

Castle Street House (The Keep)

in a chemist shop in Bath Street in 1845, when they set up a small press in the

Lamb and Fountain Inn

yard of the Wheatsheaf nearby to print labels. By 1854 they were taking on so much printing work that it was necessary to move to an outbuilding of Castle Street House (The Keep). In the following year Butler started the Somerset and Wilts Journal, which survived until 1925, when it was merged with the Somerset Standard. In 1863 Joseph Tanner was taken on as a partner and by 1892 the firm employed about 500 people. In the early 20th century the need for expansion resulted in the construction of a purpose built factory at Adderwell.

Continue along Trinity Street to Castle Street. At the corner of Trinity Street and Castle Street is the 17th century Keep, formerly the Cottage Hospital. Its outstanding 18th century elevation is the earliest example of brickwork in Frome.

Turn left down Castle Street, noticing the 17th century Lamb and Fountain Inn on the right.

Plaque 16 *16 Whittox Lane. Walk a little way to your left up Milk Street.* Number 45 was built in 1680 by Lewis Cockey.

Cockey Lamp Post

Melrose House

COCKEYS

In the late 17th century Lewis Cockey set up a bell foundry in Bell Lane, starting a firm which lasted nearly 300 years. In the early 19th century the company branched out into cast iron working, becoming manufacturers of street furniture and one of the leading producers of gas lamps. Much of the street furniture in Frome was made by Cockeys; their name can still be found on drain covers and railings, and on the older lamp standards. Cockeys were much involved in the establishment of the Frome Gas Company in 1831, and manufactured everything from piping and fittings to gasometers. Later they became general engineers, manufacturers of steam engines, iron roof frames, and all classes of engineering and iron founders work. The works were situated in Bath Street/Palmer Street, before the company relocated in 1890 to Garston, where they had their own railway sidings.

A little way further up Milk Street stands Vallis School. Originally a Rechabite chapel it was founded as a British School in 1843; it was taken over by the County Council in 1909. *Walk back down Milk Street.* On the left, set back from the road, is the old Presbytery, once the local manor house. Adjoining it, the Irvingites built a chapel in 1843. This became a Roman Catholic church in 1854, continuing until 1929. Further downhill on the left stands 17th century Melrose House. Sun Street, on the right, is mainly 18th century and has been restored following 20 years of blight.

Monmouth Chambers

Turn left by the United Reformed Church and walk down Zion footpath, which leads to Cork Street. Turn right.

Monmouth House was built by Thomas Bunn's father. The building which stands in the garden is sometimes called a stable block, but was probably used to store cloth. Number 3 Cork Street is a fine 17th century building where the Duke of Monmouth stayed shortly before his defeat at the Battle of Sedgemoor in 1685.

SINGERS

J.W.Singer trained as a watchmaker, managing a Frome shop before branching out on his own in 1844. He started with premises in Eagle Lane, and a small forge in Justice Lane, making 'medieval metal-work in silver, brass and iron',